Anime and Color

A guide to drawing anime and using colors to bring it to life

By Ritsu Kinjo

Table of Contents

Disclaimer

While all attempts have been made to verify the information provided in this book, the author does assume any responsibility for errors, omissions, or contrary interpretations of the subject matter contained within. The information provided in this book is for educational and entertainment purposes only. The reader is responsible for his or her own actions and the author does not accept any responsibilities for any liabilities or damages, real or perceived, resulting from the use of this information.

The trademarks that are used are without any consent, and the publication of the trademark is without permission or backing by the trademark owner. All trademarks and brands within this book are for clarifying purposes only and are the owned by the owners themselves, not affiliated with this document.

You wish you could do that...

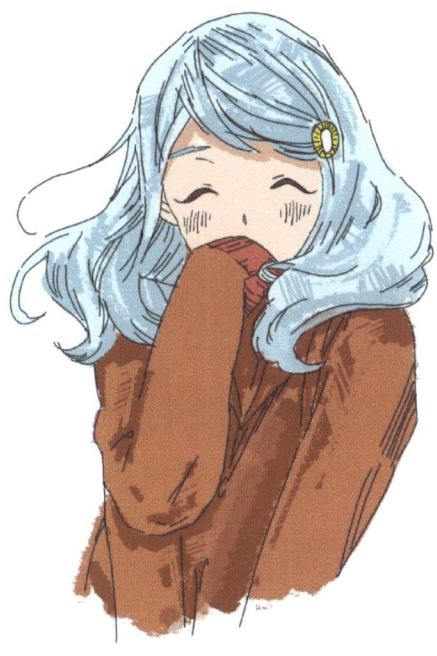

You've looked on Deviant Art. You watch all the Anime you are curious about and you've even searched and found Anime fan art. You want to draw it and use color to make it pop out of the page. So, you did what others did, you looked online for help.

You've downloaded guides and even went to bookstores to get started. You've been on YouTube to try and get little tips and tricks to put you on the path to making fantastic looking anime art, but you can't quite get there. It's frustrating. You just want a guide to explain and walk you through the process.

I get it, and that's why I have made this book, to give you the steps you need in a format that is easy to follow and encouraging as well. I will walk you through the steps to help you learn the techniques you need to draw your favorite Anime, and even maybe come up with some of your own.

You're ready to start drawing Anime...

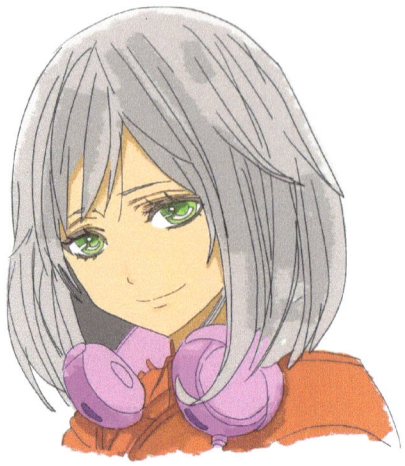

Once you purchase this book and cycle through the pages, you will find information presented in an easy to follow format. I will not only walk you through the lessons; I will also give you advice on:

1. Different types of Anime

2. Tools needed to get started in your new interest.

3. Advice on how to get into the right frame of mind.

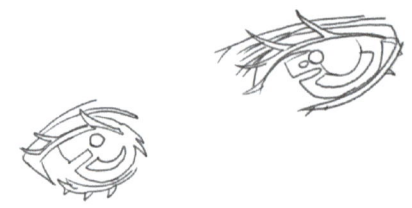

4. Techniques to help you format your pictures.

5. Tips and tricks on how to position facial features.

This book is designed to help you for when you're feeling frustrated and stuck. Learning a new interest isn't easy when you first start out, and I want to help guide you through the process. The simple and detailed steps in each lesson break down the picture to make it easier for you to follow?

Are you ready? Let's get started.

Chapter 1 – We grew up with them...

Ah, Saturday morning cartoons, a bowl of cereal, and immersing ourselves until lunch, that was the most of our childhood, and it was good. We even couldn't wait to get home from school and watch afternoon cartoons. Our lives were filled with colorful characters with goofy and serious attitudes. We couldn't wait to watch Bugs, *He-man,* and the *Super Friends*.

Then we turned on the television that fateful Saturday and were introduced to *Voltron*. It was a cartoon the likes of which we had never seen before. That's because it was Anime, Japanese Animation, and it captured our hearts and imaginations. We started looking for other Anime and found a few more. It wasn't until we connected to the internet that we were inundated with more Anime than we could imagine.

Anime spanned many genres. It brought new worlds and concepts to life. We found ourselves falling in love with Naruto and Inuyasha and pulling out the tissues when something happened to our favorite Anime characters.

Chapter 2 – Your shopping list

You've probably started out with notebook paper and a regular pencil or a mechanical one, and that's good to get your feet wet, but if you're serious about wanting to learn the nuances of drawing and coloring anime, you're going to need a few more things.

Pencils

As you already know, you can get mechanical and traditional lead and wood pencils. The traditional pencils can come in a variety of leads ranging from soft lead to the firmest lead you can find.

Below is a description of the two different types of lead.

- H- Hard lead. This is good for light sketches and getting a general idea of what you what your toon to look like, but don't bear down too hard. It will leave ruts in the paper that will not come out.

- B-Soft lead. It can erase easily, but if you layer it to make it darker, you may find yourself leaving stains on the paper. This hardness is used mainly for shading.
  You can find boxed sets of these pencils at any hobby and art store.

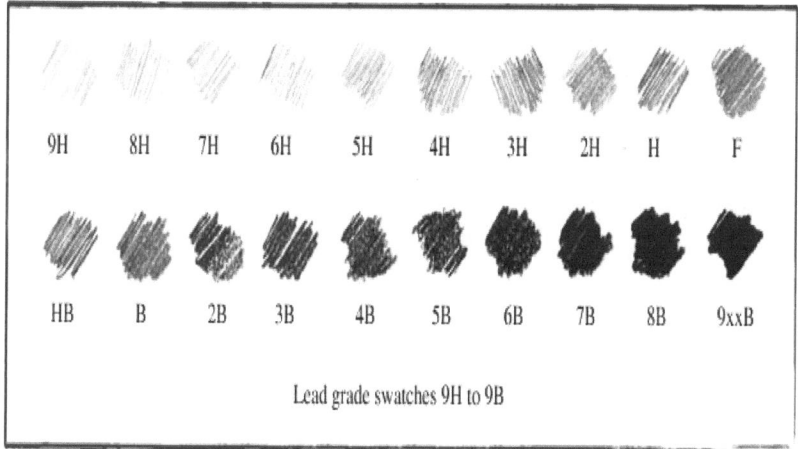

Lead grade swatches 9H to 9B

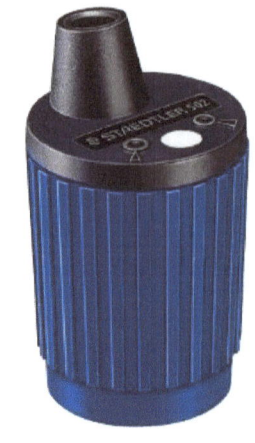

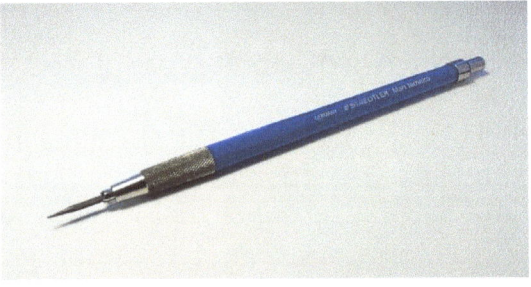

There are some artists that prefer the lead holder you see to the left. This lead holder is made of metal and can last indefinitely, making it the perfect choice for the environmentally conscious. You can buy packs of lead in different degrees of hardness, just like traditional pencils.

Pencil Sharpeners

A tool everyone has in their home already.

To the left is a lead pointer. This little gadget sharpens the lead in lead holders. All you have to do is put the lead while it is in the holder into the large hole and turn in a circular motion. The white disk you see is to take the excess lead shavings off of the lead.

Erasers

There are many erasers that artists use for various reasons, but you only really need a pink one to get started in earnest.

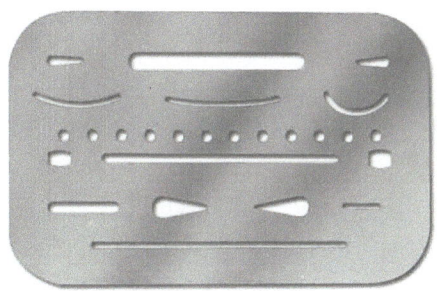

Eraser guard

As you layout and sketch your piece, you're inevitably going to have lines you don't want. This is where the little piece of metal to the left comes in to save the day. The holes have been stamped into this to help you cover the lines you want to keep and erase the lines you don't.

Paper

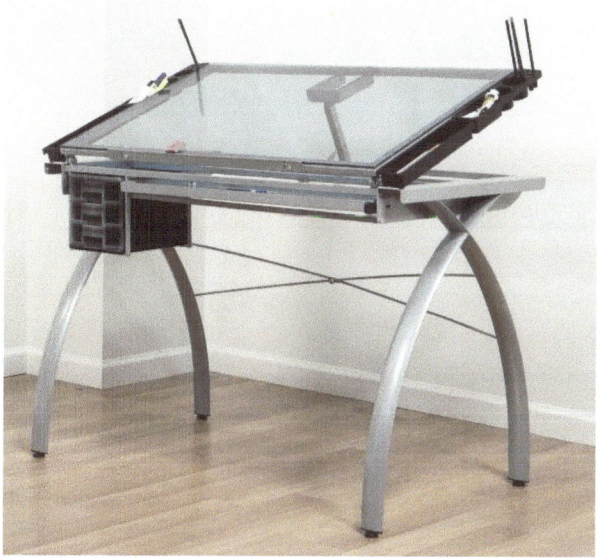

There are many different types of art paper you can use to draw and color Anime, but starting out with a standard sketch pad will be good enough for now. When you make a decision on how you wish to color your pieces in the future, you can decide on whether you are going to need thicker paper for acrylic, watercolor, or charcoal.

Your work space

You need a workspace that is comfortable and functional. It needs to be ergonically correct to reduce back and leg pain and also be versitile enough for you to adjust the height of the equipment you are using. To your left is a standard drafting table which can serve the purpose well. There are also desk chairs which can compliment this type of table.

T-square

A T-square can help you make straight lines and also keep also keep your piece level on the work surface. You can use a T-square to level templates, rulers and other tools as well.

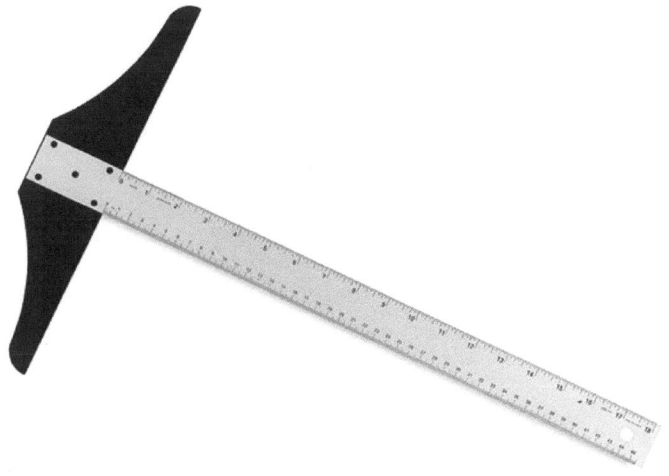

Templates

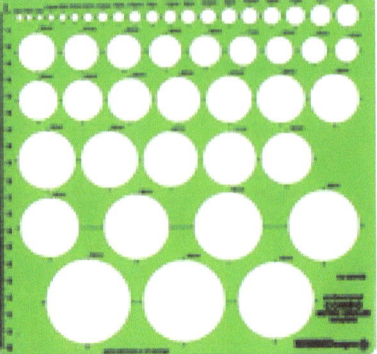

There are many features on Anime characters that can be easily and quickly drawn with the use of templates. You can find these in hobby and office supply stores.

Felt or fine tip marker

To your left are inking markers. These can help you make the pencil markings permanent once you're happy with your finished piece before you color it. There are many other brands of inking markers. I just put a picture of the most popular one here.

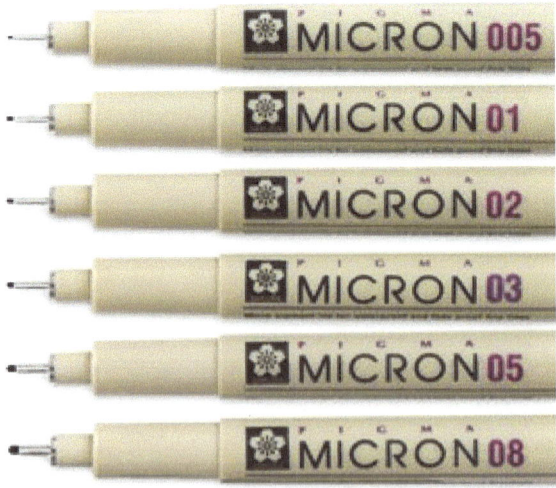

Choosing your colour medium

When you are ready to color your pieces of art, you can choose from color pencils, watercolor, acrylic, and charcoal. Each medium has a different look and feel to it. Most start with color pencils to accustom to blending colors and shading them as well.

Chapter 3 – Theory of color

Form the sky to the ground, the world is full of color. When we were little coloring books were fun. We loved to take our crayons and full those empty pictures with all the colors we could think of, but we never gave it thought of how all those colors worked together. We were young, it was fun. Now that we are older and have taken an interest in art, we find ourselves taking a closer look at how different colors work together to make a piece of art to capture the soul.

It's basic at the start.

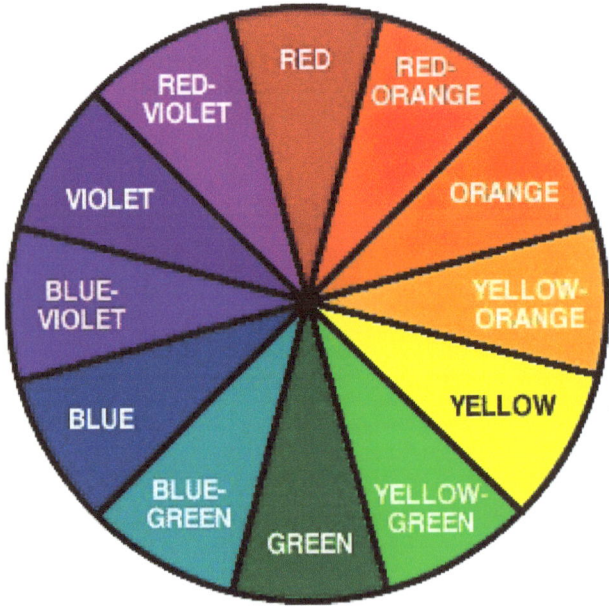

Below is a basic color wheel. These wheels help us understand how one color fades into another, how they complement each other, and how they contrast one another.

Primary colours

We are taught primary colors are blended to make other colors, and these were blue, red, and yellow, but on the color wheel, we have to more: violet and green. Though these two are made from combining the traditional primaries, these are the base colors for those combinations and that is why there are listed as primary on a color wheel.

Secondary colours

These are the colors directly to the right of the primary color. Take a good look at the secondary color. It is slightly lighter or darker depending on the color itself. This is how you can add shading your piece without having to figure out how to work in grays.

Tertiary colours

These are the one to the left of the primary. They also help you combine colors for highlighting or shading.

Complimentary and contrasting colors

Complimentary colors are the secondary and tertiary colors. They work with the primary color to add depth to a piece. Contrasting colors are the colors directly across from the primary and other colors. These colors provide you with the ability to make details in piece to stand out and be noticed.

To the left is a more expanded version of the color wheel above. This is you help you get a better idea of how artists get the different tones of flesh and other colors.

For this book, we will be using the simplified one above.

Colour equals character

Not many people take this into consideration, but here are some questions to get you thinking.

Would Naruto still be expected to be hyperactive and unique if he didn't have that shock of blond hair and wear his signature orange?

Would you expect Renji to jump into a fight instinctively if his hair wasn't red?

When coloring Anime characters, the palette you use can make all the difference.

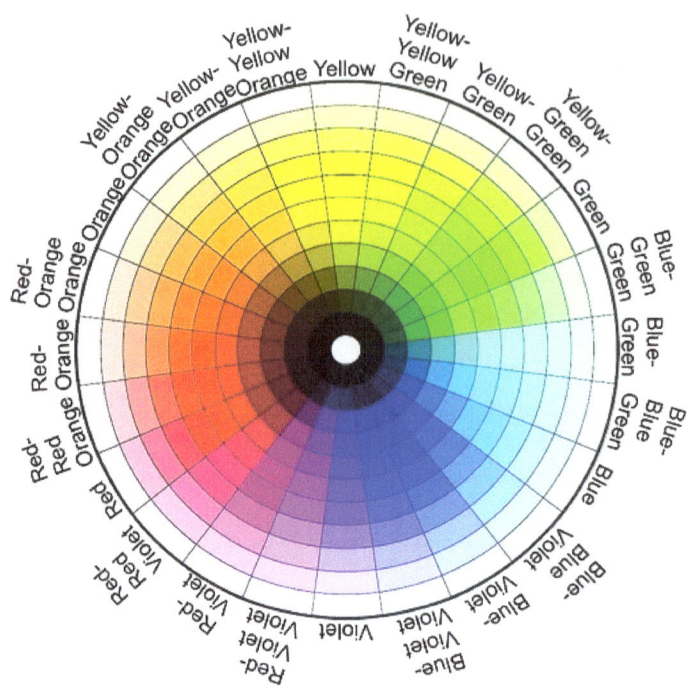

Chapter 4 - Some friendly advice...

We are all excited to start a new hobby, and learning to draw is no exception. We want to learn and jump right into it. There are some things we tend to forget.

1. It takes time to draw well.

    a. Drawing develops fine motor and muscle memory skills. It is going to take more than a few minutes to draw anything. Prepare for a lesson to take an hour at the very least.

2. Take breaks if you need them.

    a. If you come to a place to stop between steps and feel you need a break to get up and stretch. Do it. Our bodies are made to move around, and sitting for too long can lead to stiffness in the neck and shoulder area.

3. Everyone started somewhere.

    a. Don't get discouraged if your early pieces don't look anything like the artwork you see online. They all started where you are now. What you're seeing is the result of years of practice in their chosen art field. You'll get there.

Chapter 5 – A study of the face.

In order to draw the human form in any genre, you must first learn how to place the features on the face and how to tilt the head and make it believable. It can simply be one of the most taxing parts of drawing Anime or any type of humanoid character.

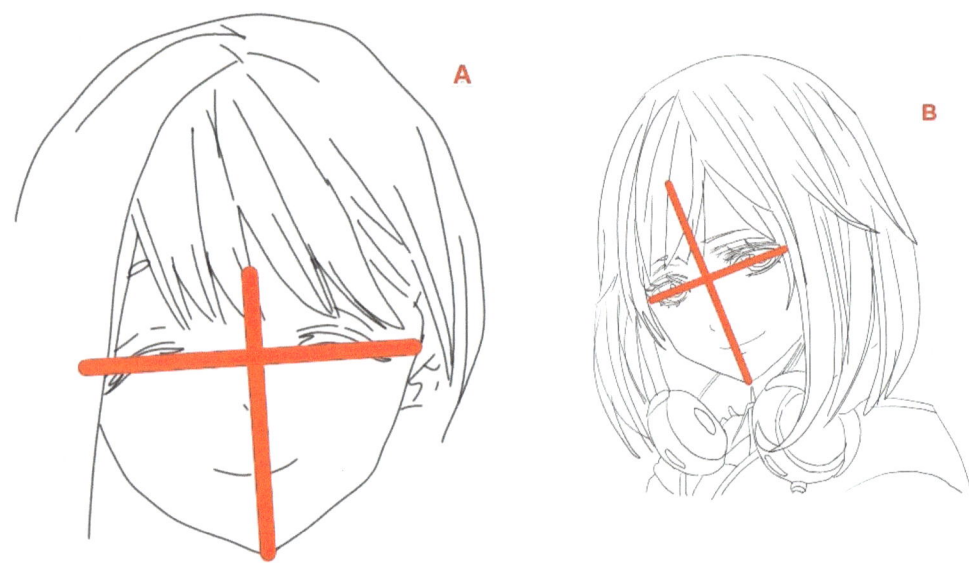

Figure A: This is a basic way to draw the head and facial features. The "T" is a trick artists use to properly align the eyes, nose, and mouth to the forehead and chin.

Figure B: I've tiled the "T" to the left. Just doing this has changed the orientation of the face, but we can still see both eyes completely.

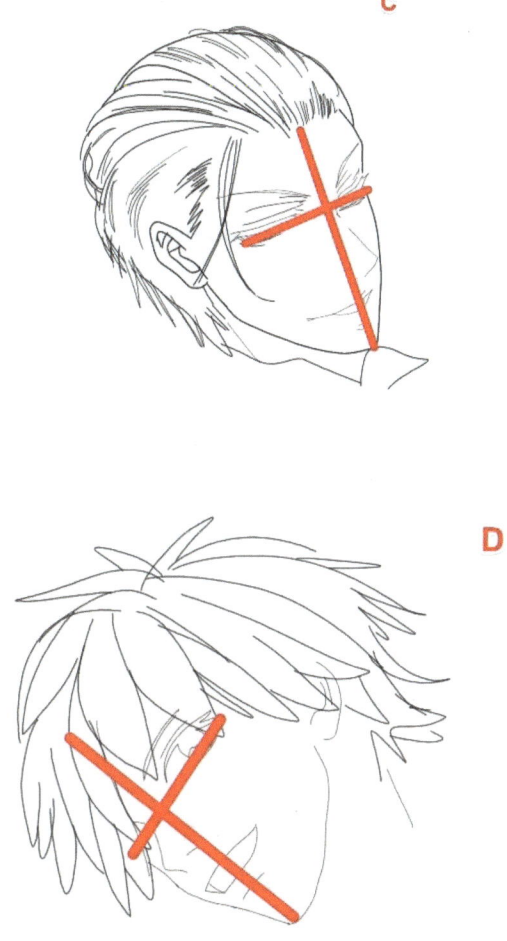

Figure C: I've learned the "T" back slightly and tiled it a little bit away from us. Notice how the right arm of the "T" is shorter? This is foreshortening. You can still see some of the eye on the right, but it looks narrower than the eye on the left.

Figure D: I've learned the "T" forward and tiled it inward. We can see how it tilts the whole head and almost completely hides and left side of the face.

Chapter 6 – A simple face

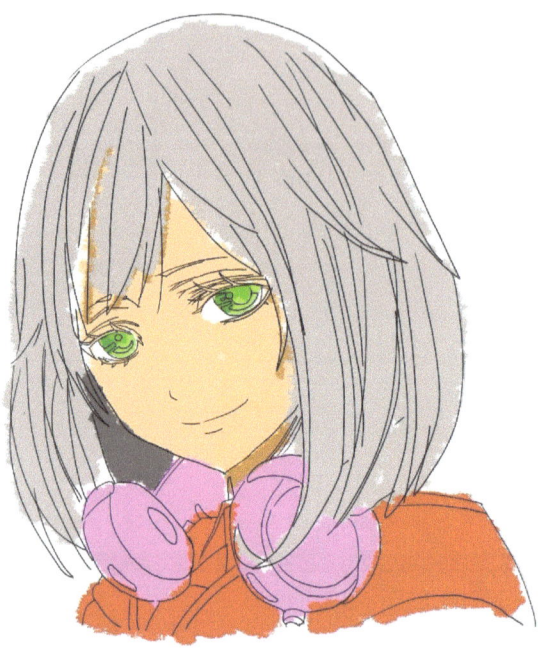

Here is one of our girls from the precious lesson. She's fully fleshed out here and even has headphones. She has a soft smile and her eyes even seem to be smiling.

After drawing you're "T", draw the inside of the eyes by first making circles.

1. Add the details of the cornea to your picture.

2. Draw the almond shape for the eye around the corneas.

3. Use sweeping curves for the lashes.

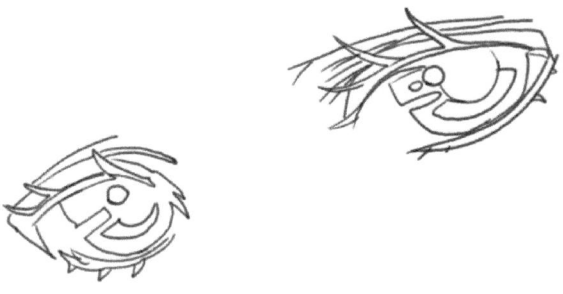

4. Use a 3/4 half-formed rectangle for the top lid.

5. Finish the eyes of by drawing curves as you seen them in the picture.

6. Add the brows.

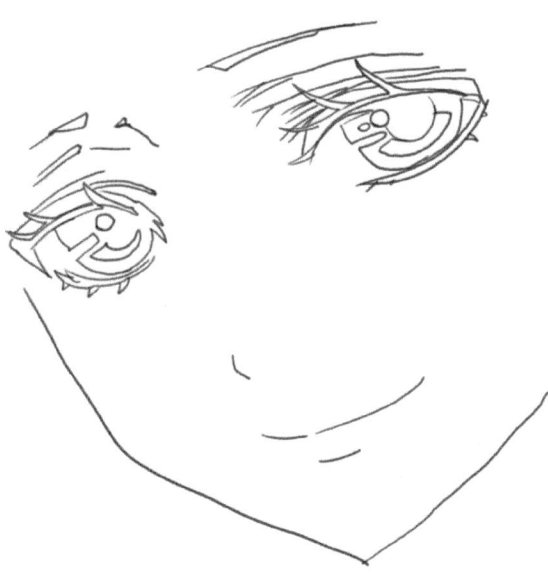

7. To start the head, make the short curve first.

8. Starting from the outside of the lft eye, make the left curve and end it by meeting the first curve you drew.

9. Make a small curve for the nose.

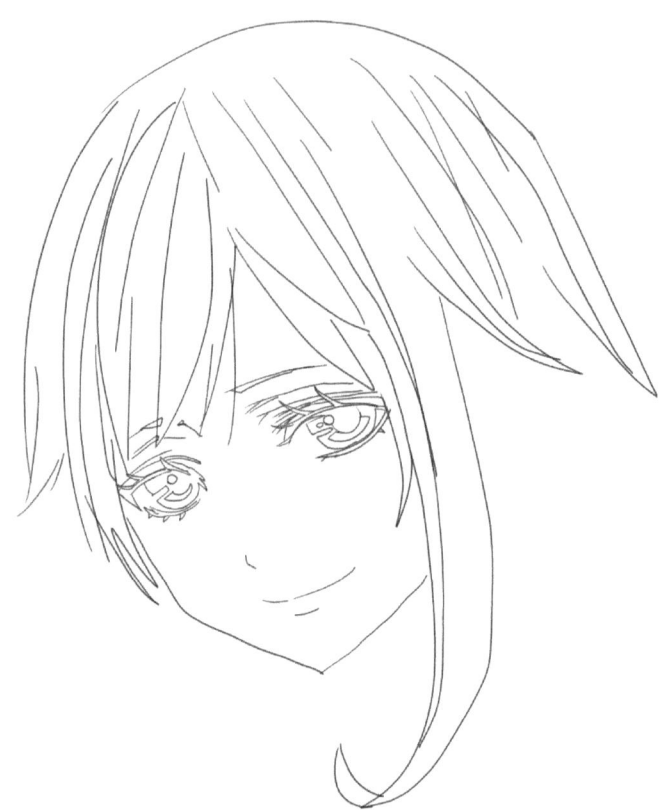

10. Make the curves for the mouth and bottom lip.

11. Start with the large curve for the top of the head.

12. Use long, sweeping curves for the longer parts of the hair.

13. Use short curved and straight lines for the shorter portions of hair.

14. Add the hair on the left side by using long curves.

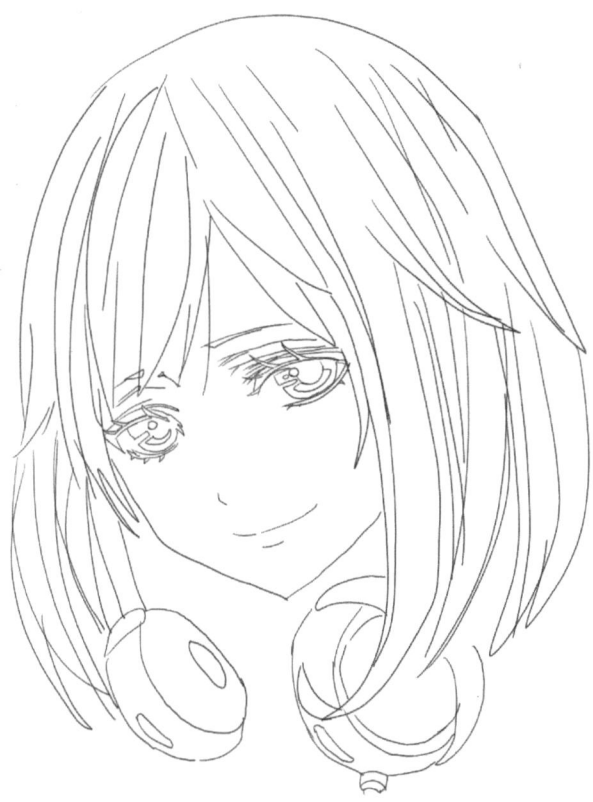

15. Starting on the left, make a loose circle for the first ear piece to the headphones.

16. Make two more curves, one directly connected to the first circle you made and one connected to the first curve you drew.

17. Add the little accents.

18. Now, draw the two curves

19. you see going up from the headphones.

20. The second half of the headphones is another series of curves. If you have a circle template or even one that helps with ellipses, they may come in handy here.

21. Focusing on the shoulder area, start on the right side by drawing the curve in the rear and then adding the three that are coming from it.

22. Continue the curves from the headphones to the edge of your paper as you see it in the picture.

23. Add the curves on the left for the other arm and shirt. Take your time.

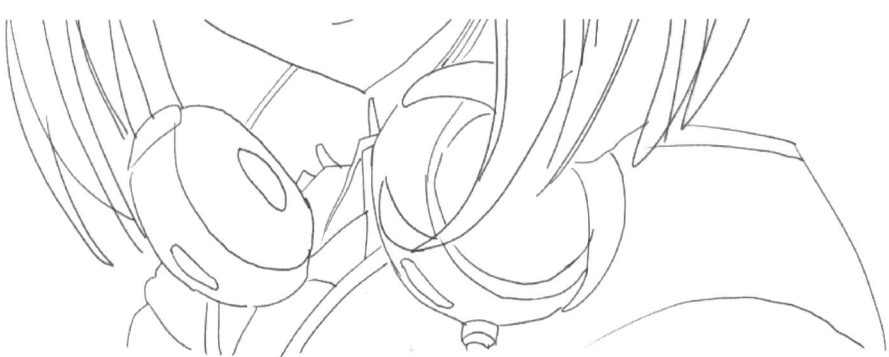

24. Using a flesh tone, color in the face.

25. Use a darker flesh tone to shade in the neck.

26. Use two different shades of green for the eyes.

27. Light lavender for the hair.

28. Darker shade of lavender for the hair in shadow.

29. A periwinkle for the headphones.

30. A shade of brown for the shirt.

31. Color in the rest of the eye with white.

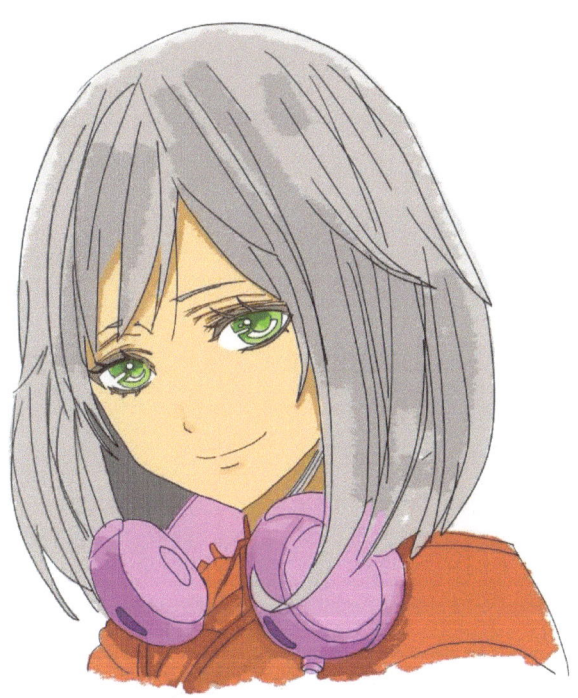

32. Using our color theory, use varying lighter shades of green to get the glossy look you see in the picture.

33. Use darker tones of flesh to shade where the hair casts a shadow.

34. Vary the shade of lavender in the hair to give it a little more depth.

35. Use a darker periwinkle to shade the headphones.

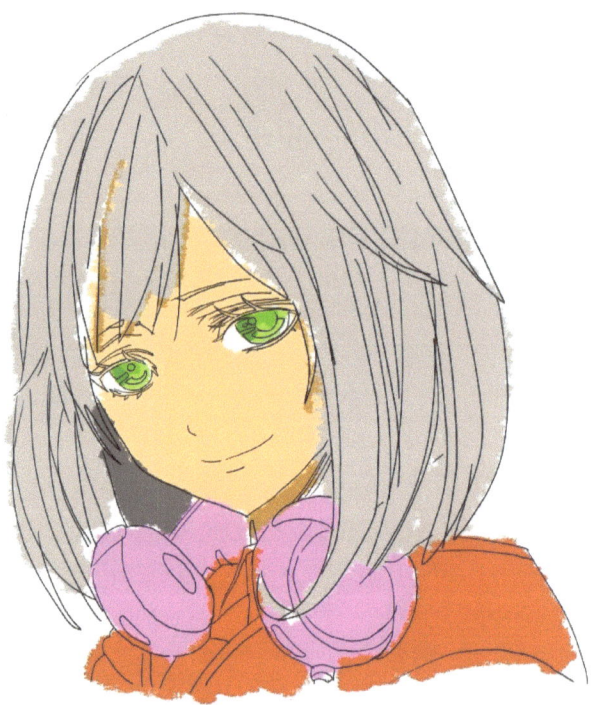

36. Use a darker tone of brown to the casted shadows of the headphones.

Bonus Lesson

Start the lesson over. How would draw it differently? How would you color it differently?

Chapter 7 – Just a little tilted

Remember this guy? We first met him in chapter 5 on how to align the facial features. We're going to flesh him out in this chapter.

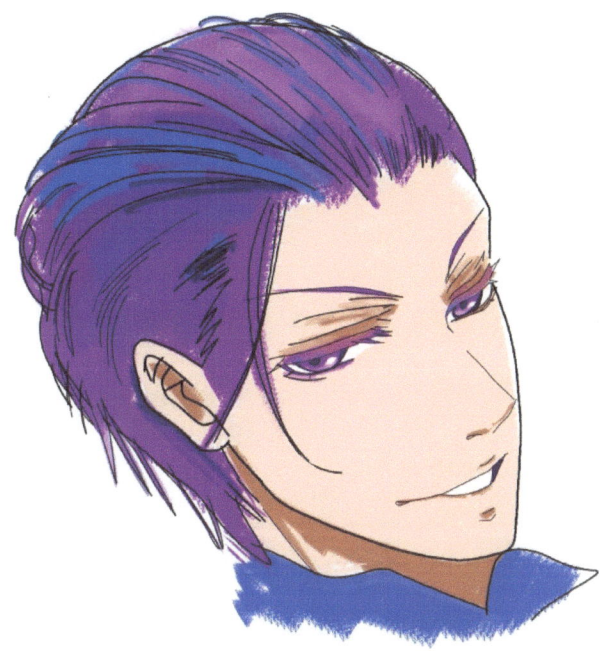

1. After you have drawn your "T", start with the eye furthest from you.

2. Make the curve for the bottom lid first.

3. Draw the inside of the eye.

4. Draw the upper lid.

5. Add the lashes and brow lines.

6. Make the curve for the bridge of the nose.

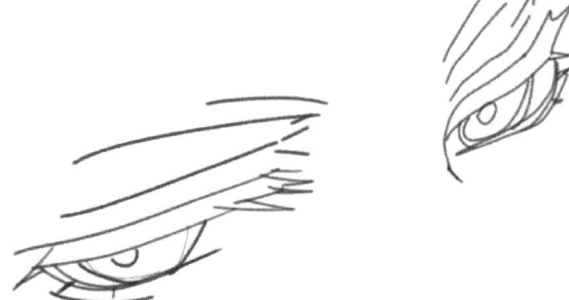

7. Duplicate steps 1-5 for the eye closest to you.

8. Add in out eyebrows.

9. Finish the nose by making an "L" shape.

10. The nostril you see is a small teardrop.

11. A small curve hints at the space just under the nose.

12. Make the top lip.

13. Draw the curve you see for the bottom lip.

14. Draw a curve on the inside of the mouth for the tongue.

15. Take this time to double check your work.

16. Draw the curves for the right side of the face.

17. Draw the jaw line as a sweeping curve coming down from just below the left eye.

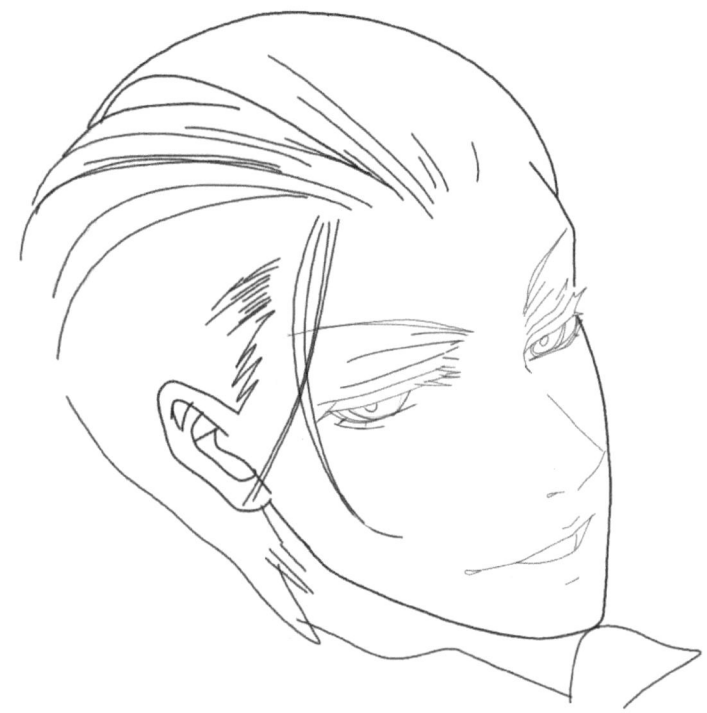

18. Make a series of curves for the outer part of the ear.

19. Draw the curves you see for the rest of the ear from the outside inward.

20. Make your large curve for the top of the head.

21. Make the other curves to finish the hair on the top of the head.

22. Make another curve with a few bumps for the back of the hair.

23. Make a zig-zag to start the side burn.

24. Make quick hash marks for the rest of the side burn.

25. The collar is just some simple curves.

26. I've added a little more hair in this step. Compare what you have so far to this step and fill in your picture.

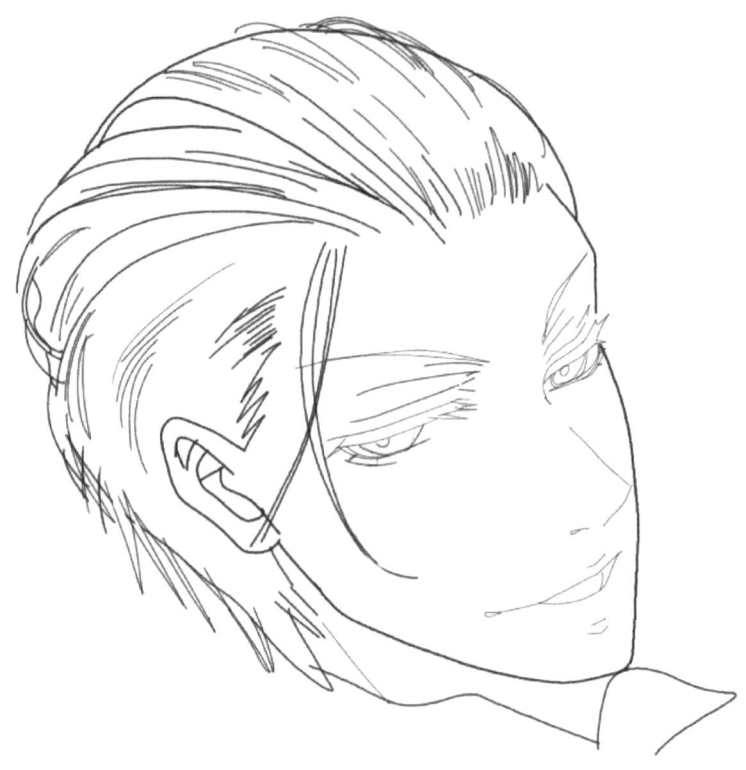

27. I used purples and blues for his hair and eyes.

28. I used a lighter flesh tone than the last lesson to make him appear pale.

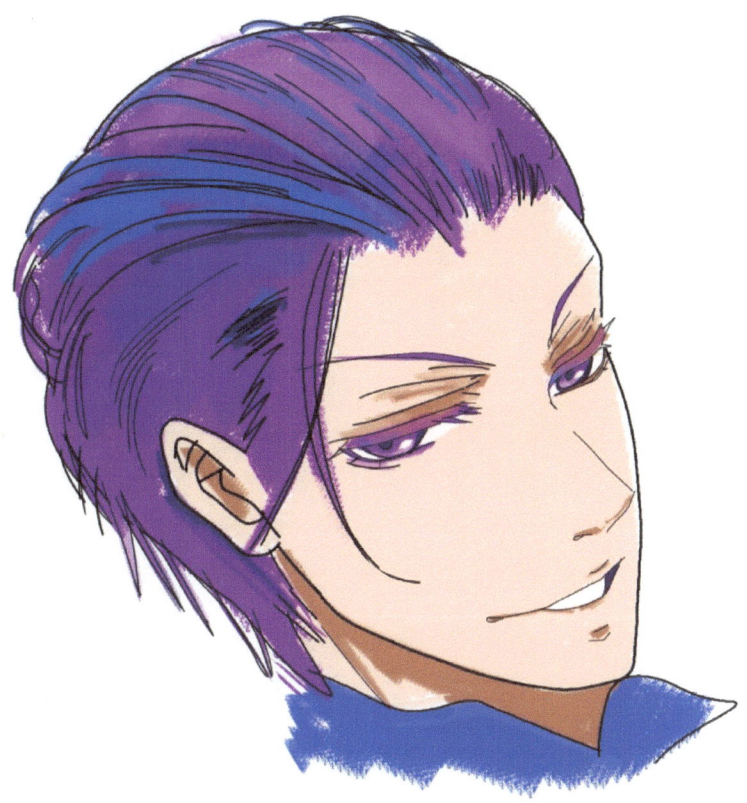

29. I used the blue from the hair for his shirt.

30. Again, I used darker tones of the colors for the shading effects.

Chapter 8 - Girl in a sweater

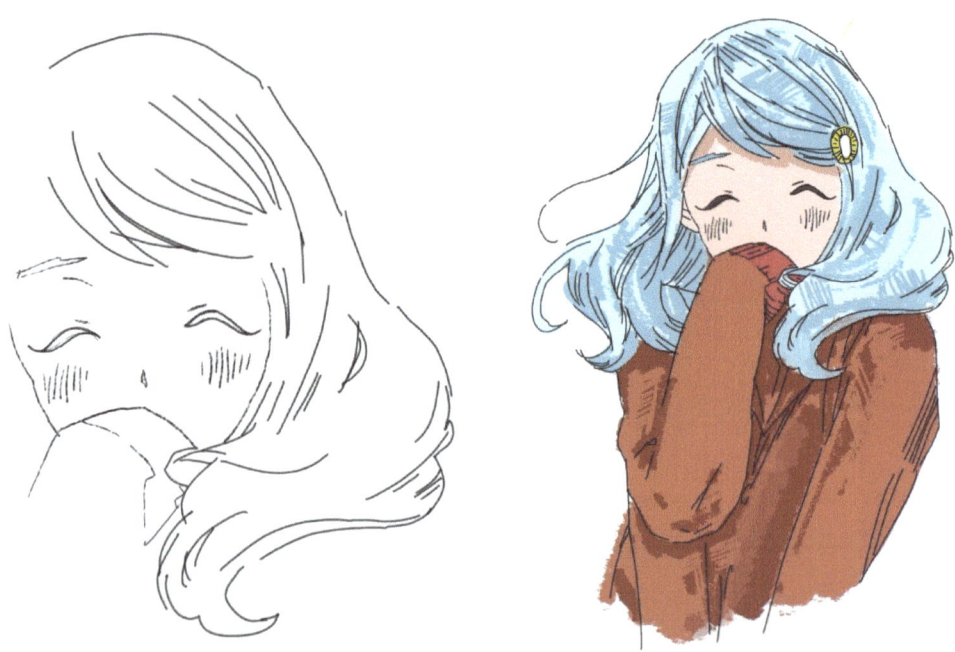

I decided this lesson should have a little more to it. Even though her eyes are closed and her mouth is covered, I will be walking you through how to draw her figure. You will notice there are more shaded spots on her. This is mainly due to how the fabric lays on her body.

1. Start by drawing the curves for her eyes.

2. Add the little triangle for her nose.

3. Add in the accents around the eyes.

4. Add the eyebrow.

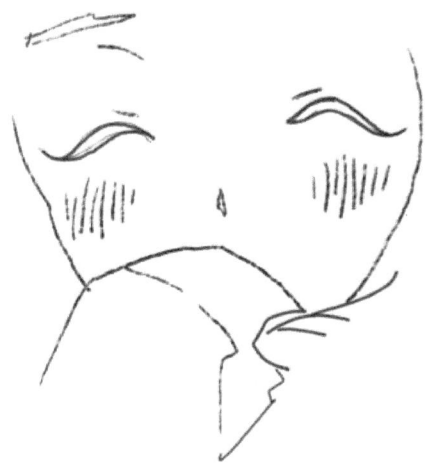

5. Draw the hash marks for her cheeks.

6. Draw the curves to frame her face.

7. Draw the collar coming from the right side of her neck.

8. Draw the soft, wide angle for her cuff.

9. Follow it up by draw the curves for the sleeve.

10. Make the large curves to outline the shape of the head.

11. Continue by drawing long, sweeping curves for the hair as you see in the picture.

12. Make the rest of the curves for the hair.

13. Don't forget the sharp angles for the shoulder and start of the sweater.

14. On the left side of the head, add a curve and a couple of hash marks for the ear you can see.

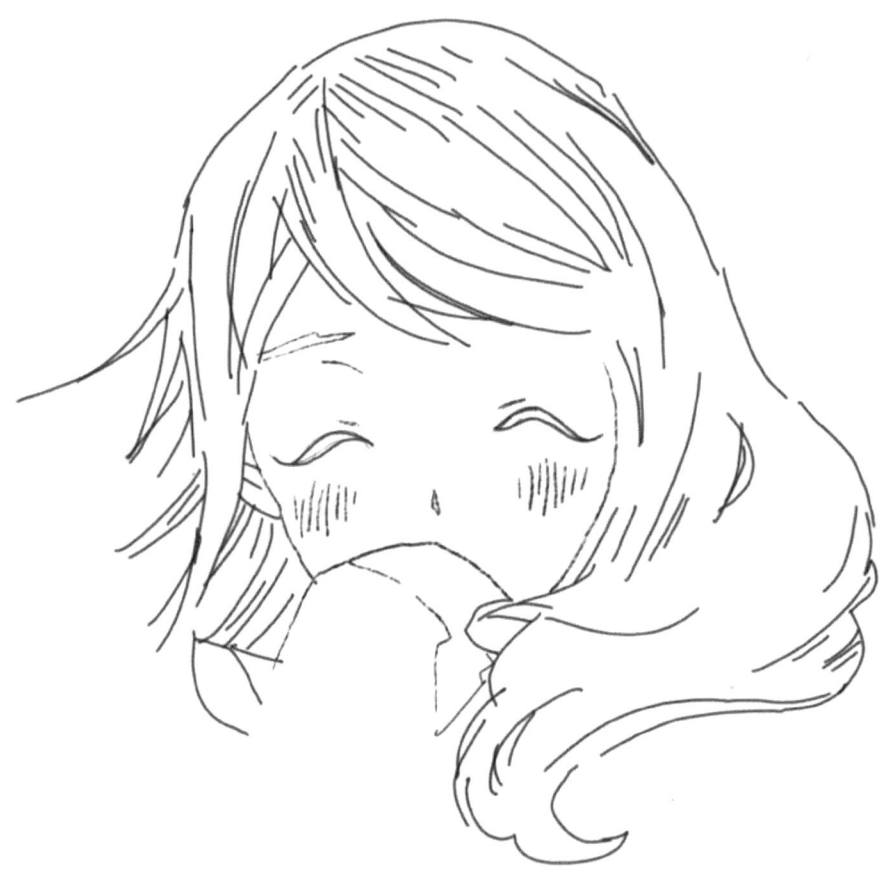

15. Add the fly-away parts for the hair.

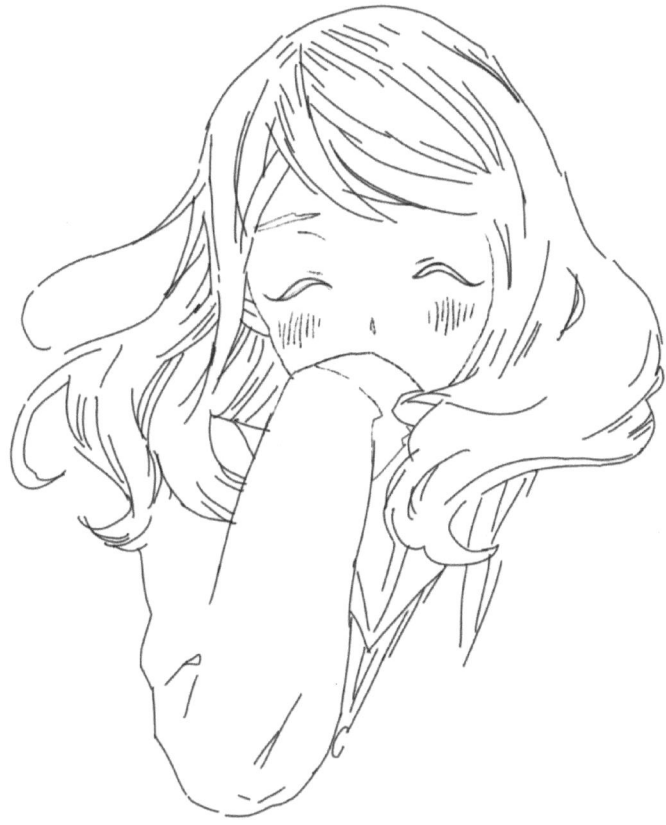

16. Finish the hair on the left side.

17. From the last curl on the left side, make the curve for her arm.

18. Coming down from her face, make the lines that connect the sleeve on the left side first.

19. Bring the right side down.

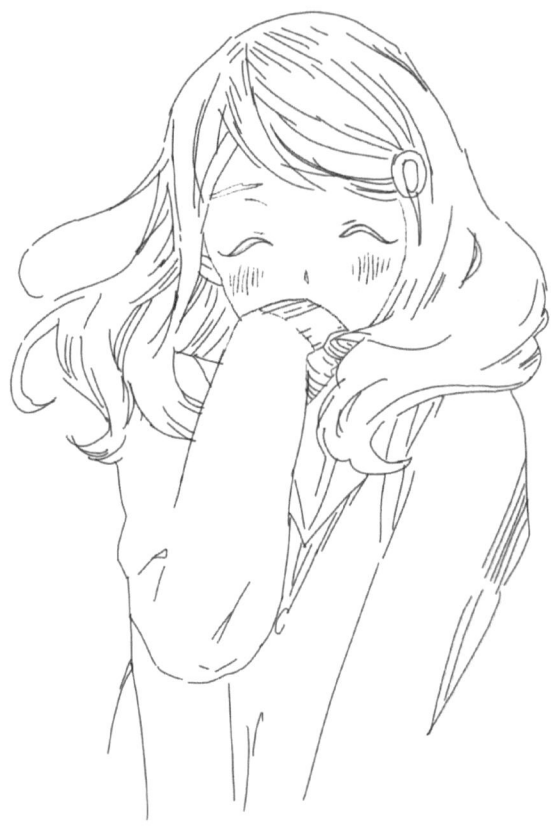

20. Make the "V" shapes you see for the front of the sweater.

21. Don't forget the hash marks on the front of the sweater and the sleeve.

22. In space we left close to the right temple, draw one circle in another to make the hair clip.

23.   Bring the rest of the sweater down on the left by drawing sweeping curves.

24.   Follow the lines you started on the right to finish of that side of our character.

Take this time to compare and see if there is anything that was missed before we add the color. You're doing well. Remember, take your time.

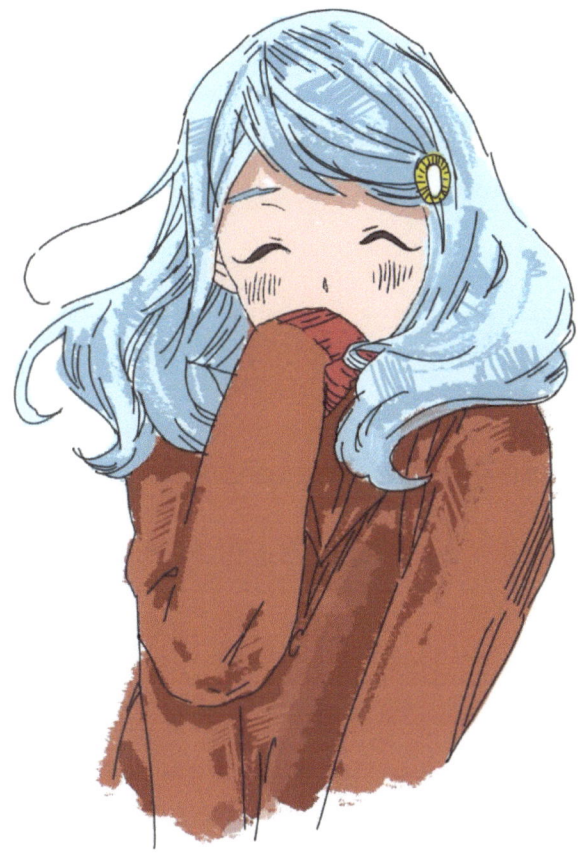

For the colors, we used two different flesh tones, one for the main color of her complexion and one for the shading. We used a sky blue and a slightly darker blue for the highlights and shading. We used a king's gold for the hair clip and two shades of brown for her sweater.

Bonus Lesson

Draw her again. How would draw her differently? What colors would you use?

Chapter 9 - A different pose

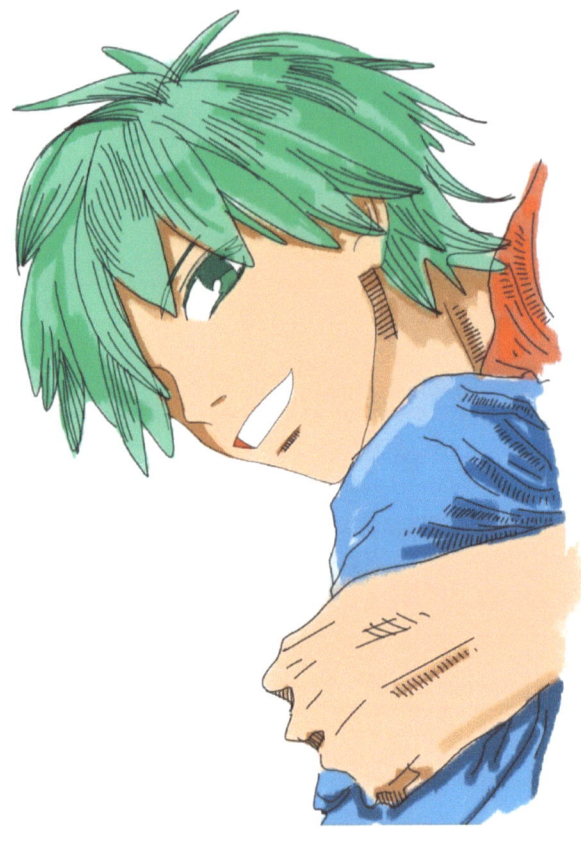

Here we have a young man grabbing his leg. One of his eyes is covered by his hair, and you can see his hand and leg. It looks like he's getting ready to run somewhere doesn't it? How you pose someone can give hints as to their intensions, and in this one, he looks ready for action. The smile on his face tells us he's having fun. I am sure you've noticed the lack of detail in regards to the teeth. If you were to draw lines going up to the gum line, it would not look natural. So, just highlighting the teeth in a solid white is good enough.

1. Remember your "T"? Draw it first.

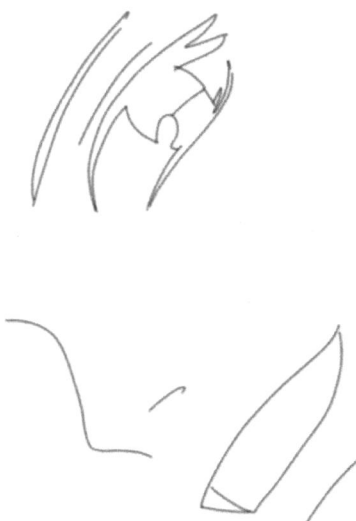

2. Draw the eye on the crossbar. Start with the inside of the eye and work your way out.

3. Add the line above the eye.

4. Add the eyebrow.

5. Make the nose by drawing a curved "L" and small check mark.

6. The mouth is in a "D" shape.

7. Make a line for the teeth.

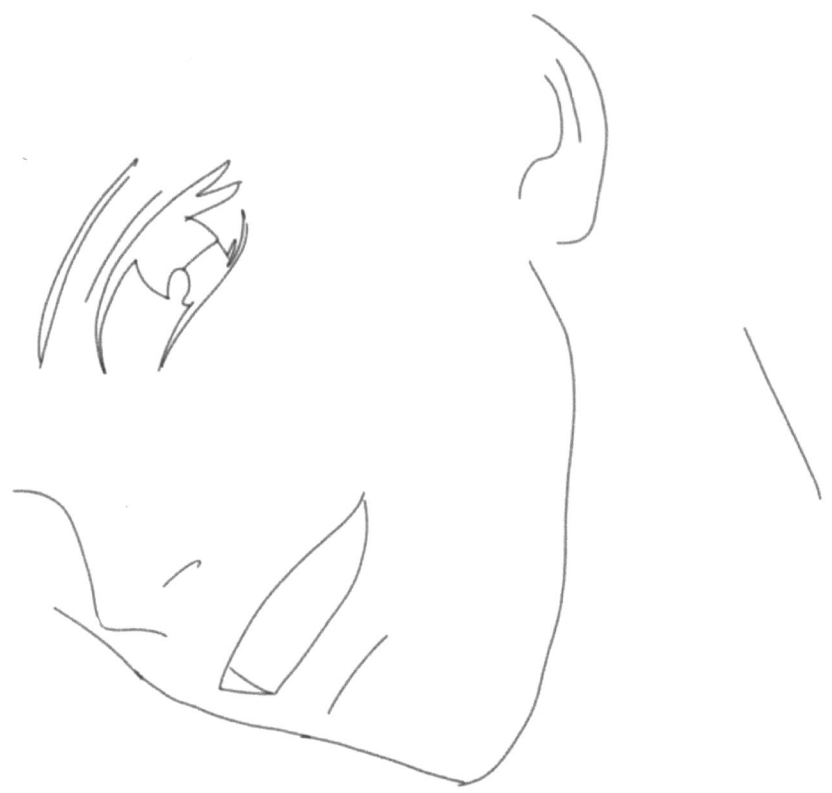

8. Add the line for under the bottom lip.

9. Align the ear with the eyebrow.

10. Make the outer curve first.

11. Add the line and second curve of the ear.

12. Make the line for the neck.

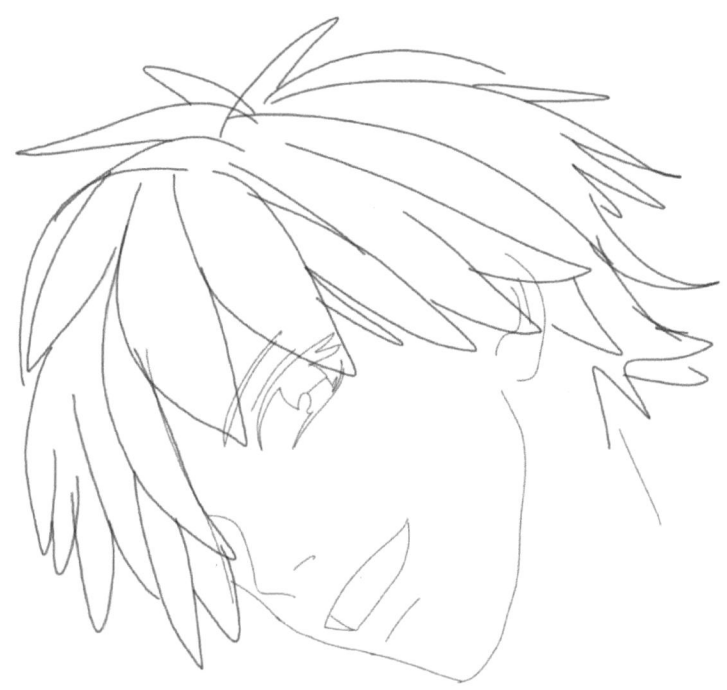

13. Make the curve for the face starting from the ear and work your way down the jawline.

14. Draw the left part of the face and stop when it forms the chin.

15. To make the hair, start with the front of the head, and make pointed "U" shapes and work your way to the back of the head.

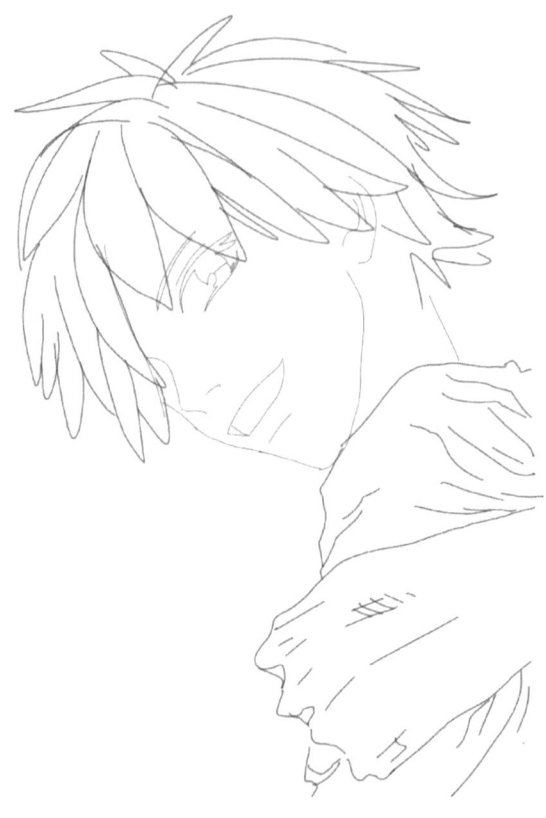

16. For the back of the head, make a sweeping curve and then curves ending them in points.

17. Starting with the pant leg, draw the crooked curve coming in from the side of your piece. Stop when you get to where the hand should be.

18. To draw the hand, start with where the thumb should be, and make a curved line that stops where the top of the leg starts.

19. Make a wavy line for the knuckles.

20. Finish it with another wavy ending where the first one did.

21. Finish the edge of the pant leg.

22. Fill in the wrinkles of the pant leg above the hand.

23. Make the lines on the hand as you see them in the picture.

24. Finish the pant leg.

25. Come up from the pant leg and add in the shirt by making a curved line.

26. Add the hash marks on the clothing.

27. Add the lines in the hair to fill it in..

Take this time to compare what you have done and see if you have missed anything.

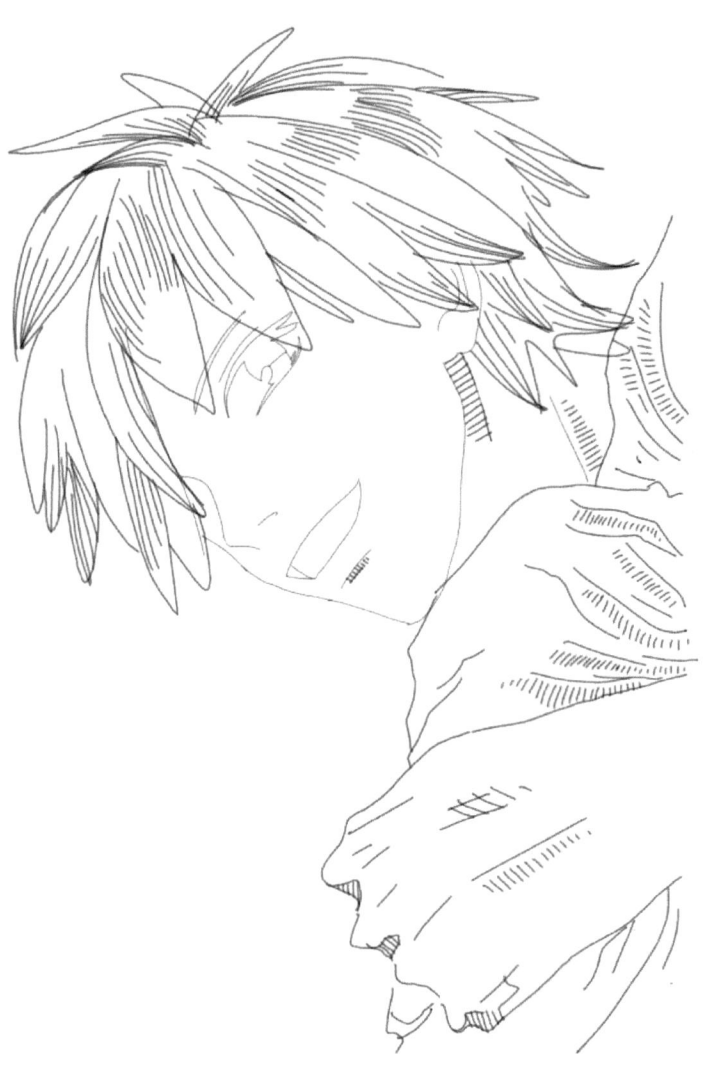

We used mint and other light greens for the hair and eyes, white for the main part of the eyes and teeth. We used to different flesh tones for the skin, two different shades of blue for the pants, and two reds for the shirt.

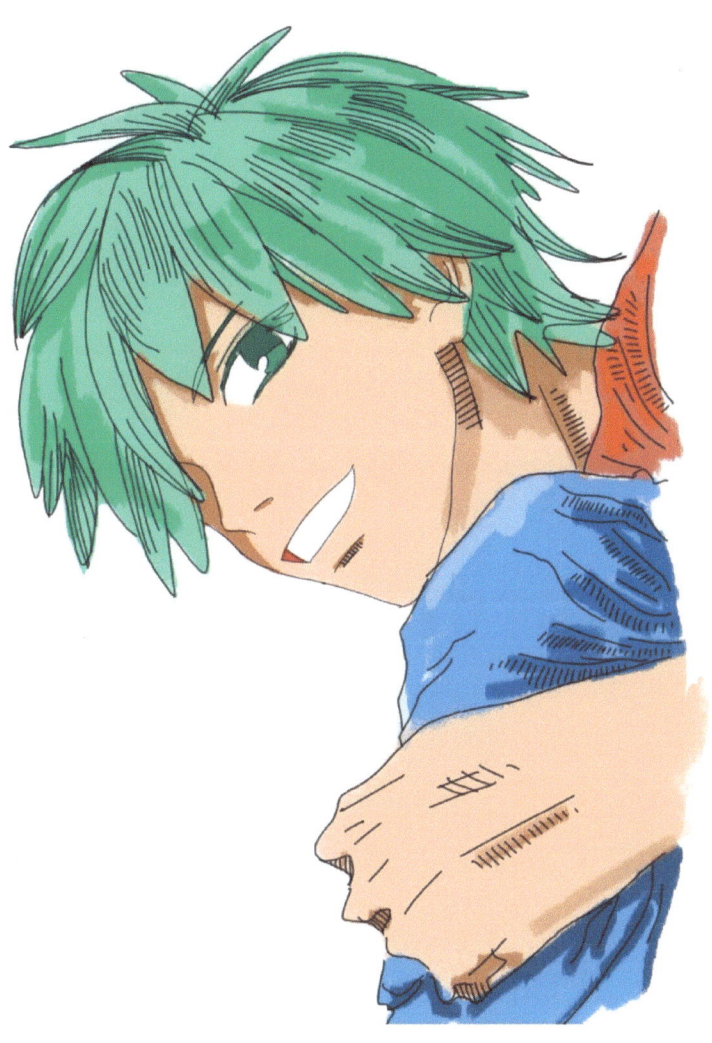

Final Words

Learning how to add color to your works of art can be fun and rewarding. In your spare time, take a sketch pad and just toy around with different shades of the same color and see what you can come up with and how you can apply those colors to future pieces. Keep practicing and never lose the passion.

Thank you!

Thank you for choosing our book, we hope you found it interesting and helpful.

If you liked the book, please give us a favor to write your review.

We would really appreciate this!

If you would like to have a bonus – **FREE BOOK**, please send the screenshot of your review to this e-mail: **gloria.kemer@gmail.com** and we will send you a **FREE BOOK** in PDF as a **GIFT!****

Hope to see you in our future books and good luck in your drawing experience!

** in the e-mail subject please mention the name of the book you reviewed and the author.

www.ingramcontent.com/pod-product-compliance
Lightning Source LLC
Chambersburg PA
CBHW050824180526
45159CB00004B/1777